Original title:
The Brooch of Light

Copyright © 2025 Creative Arts Management OÜ
All rights reserved.

Author: Charles Whitfield
ISBN HARDBACK: 978-1-80586-137-9
ISBN PAPERBACK: 978-1-80586-609-1

A Pendant's Promise

Once I found a shiny thing,
It made my heart take wing.
A pendant dancing in the sun,
I thought, 'What joy, I've finally won!'

It promised magic, bright and bold,
But turned out to be painted gold.
The sparkle caught my eye with flair,
Then flew away, I swear, I swear!

Lightweaver's Gift

A jester waved a wand so grand,
And crafted jewels with a silly hand.
Each piece a treasure, each a joke,
A laughing light, a prankster's cloak.

I wore a spark that tickled me,
And giggles flew so wild and free.
No other gift could make me chortle,
Like those bright gems from the portal!

Sparkling Echoes

In a market bustling, a sound so fine,
Echoes of laughter twisted in line.
A shimmering trinket caught my eye,
With whispers of joy, oh me, oh my!

I thought I'd found a gem of wit,
But all it did was jiggle a bit.
It winked and rolled into the street,
Chasing pigeons, oh what a feat!

Radiant Tapestry

A tapestry woven with threads of fun,
Each glimmer a story, every thread a pun.
I knitted bright tales, oh what a sight,
With laughter woven through the night.

Each stitch a chuckle, each color a glee,
A tapestry dancing, come join with me!
It wrapped us tight in a humorous hug,
Till we stumbled and fell, all snug as a bug!

The Gem of Possibility

In a drawer of dreams, it gleams bright,
A gem so odd, it gives quite a fright.
It whispers of wonders, silly and sweet,
But beware of the sock it might eat!

A chance for a joke, a giggle, a grin,
Like trying to dance with a cat that won't spin.
It promises pathways to things you can't find,
Like a cheese wheel shaped like a duck in your mind!

Aurora's Touch

With a flick of her wrist, she sprinkles some glee,
Turning broccoli into a bright, fancy tree.
Every frown transforms into bubble and bounce,
Just beware of the tickles that make your heart flounce!

In her world, the sun wears a bright silly hat,
And each cloud is a donut for hungry old cats.
Stars laugh in the night, dancing pirouettes,
While shadows form shapes of spaghetti and pets!

Shimmering Pathways

On a path made of sparkles and glittery cheer,
Unexpectedly tripping over bright rubber deer.
Each step feels like bouncing, you never will fall,
A frog in a tuxedo now is singing with all!

You might find a cupcake that offers a ride,
With sprinkles that giggle and frosting that slides.
Dance with the figures that pop from the trees,
While yelling out secrets to buzzing fat bees!

Glint of Serendipity

A glint in the corner hints mischief anew,
A chance for a laugh and perhaps a quick stew.
It catapults you into a pie-laden whirl,
While muffins juggle muffins and cookies do twirl!

In this world of confusion and silly delight,
Butterflies wear glasses to read books at night.
Each corner you turn, a surprise waits and shouts,
As lemons play hopscotch and giggle about sprout!

Dawn's Embrace

Morning yawns, a sleepy tease,
Sunbeam slides with playful ease.
Coffee spills, oh what a sight,
Who knew mugs could take to flight?

Birds are chirping, tunes off-key,
A squirrel tries to dance with glee.
Breezes giggle past my ear,
Is that a cloud? Or my last beer?

Glistening Pathways

Twinkles dance on paths so bright,
Stumbling over my own delight.
Flip-flops flapping, what a sound,
As I wander lost, but bound.

Laughter bubbles in the air,
A cat struts by without a care.
Puddles splashed, mud on my toes,
Do I walk? Or am I posed?

Shining Epiphany

Eureka shouted at a bee,
Did it just land on my knee?
Ideas buzz, they twist and twirl,
As my thoughts begin to whirl.

Then a lamp flickers, I trip and fall,
Oh, it's just a cat's soft call!
No grand insight, just feline grace,
Laughter echoes in this space.

The Light Within

Shiny things inside my head,
Mix of wisdom, jokes, and dread.
If I tickle my own thoughts,
A spark of laughter's what I've sought!

Dancing shadows on the wall,
Guess who's caught in their own sprawl?
With a wink, and a silly grin,
Who says fun can't start within?

Luminous Whispers

In a pocket, treasure rests,
Glows and giggles, what's the jest?
Does it shine to make you smile?
Or just prank us every while?

When you wear it, dance a spree,
Little quirks, so wild and free!
It whispers tales of silly glee,
Unlikely friends, it's plain to see.

Jewels of Dawn

Morning sun has plans, you bet,
Sprinkling sparkles, no regret.
Each bead a laugh, each gem a tease,
Tickles your heart, puts you at ease.

In the daylight, they play hide-and-seek,
Gems glow back, bold and cheeky streak!
They bounce around like a playful muse,
Chasing shadows, refusing to lose.

Threads of Illumination

Woven together, colors bright,
Strings of laughter, pure delight.
When you pull one, it starts the game,
All the others join in the fame.

Hola, amigo, what's your name?
Each thread a punchline; none the same!
Stitched with joy, a quirky grin,
Hold on tight, let the fun begin.

A Necklace of Stars

Around your neck, a cosmic plan,
Each star a joke, a clever ban!
Twinkling smiles up in the air,
A constellation, beyond compare.

Wobbly orbit, never straight,
These stars don't follow the usual fate.
So throw your head back, laugh out loud,
For celestial humor, we're all so proud!

Halos of Memory's Embrace

In the drawer where lost things hide,
A sock, a key, and giggles wide.
I found a halo made of fluff,
It claimed to shine, but it's just tough.

With every flip, the memories fly,
An old receipt, a cat's sly eye.
It teases me with goofy glee,
That light, my friend, is way too free.

Shards of Radiance in Time

I dropped my snack, heard a loud clink,
Was that a diamond, or just my drink?
Shards of laughter scatter around,
In the spotlight, lost snacks abound.

A twinkle here, a glimmer there,
Each crumb a story, makes you stare.
They catch the light, then run away,
Who knew my crumbs could dance and play?

A Flicker in the Fabric of Night

The stars are winking, oh what a spree,
I asked one out for tea, had to flee!
A flicker here, a giggle there,
The cosmos laughs, no time to spare.

I stitched a tale with moonlight thread,
A quilt of puns on my sleepy bed.
But in my dreams, the jokes take flight,
A silly dance in the fabric of night.

The Twinkle that Steals the Breath

Oh, that twinkle, it caught my eye,
A firefly dressed as a curious guy.
He teased the cat, bustled with flair,
While I just stood in awed despair.

With each blink, the giggles grew,
A starry prank, a lighthearted brew.
My heart raced, a fit of mirth,
He stole my breath, for what it's worth.

The Glimmering Veil

In the corner, something shines,
A little glimmer, oh how divine.
It wobbles when I take a peek,
Like a laughing friend who's shy to speak.

I questioned if it's just a trick,
A fancy gem, or just a stick?
It sparkles bright, but where's the catch?
Maybe it's hiding from the match!

It giggles softly, oh what fun,
A secret dance with everyone.
In my pocket, snug and tight,
I'll share my treasure, what a sight!

Beyond the Dim

Beyond the shadows, something gleams,
A twinkling joke from childhood dreams.
It whispers 'come, let's have some fun,'
Like a prankster under the sun.

My friends all gather, eyes astare,
What's that shimmer in the air?
A wild creature of sparkly might,
Or just my cat, in morning light?

We chase it down, we laugh and play,
It teases us, then runs away.
"Oh come on back, don't be so shy!"
It rolls as if to say goodbye.

Celestial Memories

In a jar of starlit tales,
Sparkling stories, giggly gales.
Each memory a glowing bead,
Wink and laugh with joyful speed.

I shake the jar, and out they fly,
Dancing bright across the sky.
"Hey, remember when we tripped?"
Some sparkles laugh, and others slip.

They whizz around with silly glee,
Chasing shadows, wild and free.
We twirled and whirled, what a spree,
A galaxy in revelry!

The Dance of Illumination

When lanterns sway and shadows shift,
The light begins to play a gift.
It tickles toes, it jigs and jives,
In silly ways, it brings us lives.

We twirl in circles, round and round,
Magic feet on glowing ground.
A light that giggles, chirps, and sings,
Twirling bright on hidden wings.

Oh, what a party, let's not forget,
The joy and fun we've all met!
We'll dance until the night is through,
With lights that laugh, and love that's true!

Elysian Embers

In the garden of giggles, we dance with delight,
Wearing sparkly horrors that make the night bright.
Those little shiny treasures, oh what a sight,
Tickling our fancy, they sparkle just right.

Whispers of whimsy float on the breeze,
As the fireflies laugh, with the utmost ease.
We twirl and we spin, oh, how we please,
Catching the moonlight, like a playful tease.

Celestial Lace

In a tapestry woven with laughter and cheer,
Each twinkle and spark allows our joys to steer.
Threading our stories, oh, never a fear,
Adorning ourselves in this cosmic veneer.

Stitched up in curious patterns so bright,
Shapes of laughter play in the pale moonlight.
With vibrant threads, we create our delight,
Fashioned in giggles, everything feels right.

Chasing Starlight

Wandering 'neath a sky of outrageous dreams,
Scooping up sparkles, or so it seems.
Each burst of delight, like candy it beams,
In this game of laughter, nothing redeems.

Running 'round corners, unnoticeably sly,
We grab the stars, paint them in the sky.
With twinkling eyes, we tumble and fly,
Who knew the cosmos could giggle so high?

Flicker of Inspiration

In a world of bright ideas, we jest and we shout,
The lightbulbs above us are dancing about.
Each glimmer a secret that makes us jump out,
Giggling madly, without any doubt.

Bouncing on thoughts like a frog on the ground,
Jotting down laughter, oscillating sound.
With joy as our compass, we're merrily bound,
In this flicker of nonsense, pure fun knows no bound.

Quicksilver Flickers

In a world of shiny stars,
The cat confuses it for bars.
He pounces high, then falls and slips,
Landing hard on woeful lips.

A squirrel steals the radiant gem,
Wearing it like a fluffy hem.
It twirls and spins with little care,
While birds all argue in midair.

The dog is running, tail so bright,
Chasing shadows in the night.
He thinks he's caught a twinkling dime,
But it's just an old shoe, how sublime!

So if you seek some mirthful cheer,
Just gaze upon the silly sphere.
For in each flicker, joy ignites,
And laughter dances through the nights.

Enchanted Glow

A glowing ball rolls down the stairs,
The rabbit hops, forgetting cares.
Chasing the light with endless glee,
But trips on carrots, oh dear me!

The hedgehog dons a shiny crown,
As flamingos waddle, upside down.
They stop and stare, with feathers bright,
It's a royal mishap, what a sight!

A magical cookie appears one day,
With sprinkles that dance and sway.
The mice conspire, they plan and plot,
But all they get is a cookie hot!

So let your heart embrace the fun,
With glow and giggles, never shun.
For life's a party, bright and loud,
Where silly moments make us proud.

The Illumination Token

A shiny token on a shelf,
Claims to grant wishes by itself.
But when it twinkles out of sight,
It's just a lightbulb, oh what fright!

The clever raccoon takes a peek,
Thinking it's treasure, oh so sleek.
He puts it on his head to boast,
And starts a dance, now he's the host!

A friendly owl, wise and bold,
Sees through tricks, or so he's told.
With spectacles perched upon his beak,
He hoots, "Your treasure's just a freak!"

So if you find a crazy charm,
Don't rush to wear it, cause harm.
Just giggle at the silly glow,
And let your quirks all freely flow.

Flickering Encounters

When fireflies gather for a chat,
The frog croaks loud and tips his hat.
"Who's the brightest?" he boasts with glee,
As ladybugs roll their eyes, you see.

The fox attempts to dance around,
But stumbles, lands upon the ground.
With twirls and twists, what a disguise,
A clumsy prince 'neath twinkling skies!

A raccoon with sparkly shoes,
Wants to join, but sings the blues.
His fashion sense is quite absurd,
As he wiggles like a silly bird!

So skip and leap with joy and light,
Embrace the quirks of day and night.
For in those moments, laughter's found,
In every flicker, joy abounds!

Gilded Echoes

In a world where sparkles dance,
A pin that glimmers at every chance.
It sings a tune of shimmery flair,
While people stop and really stare.

A twist of fate, or just bad luck,
It waddles like a hapless duck.
Oh, what a sight, it shines and twirls,
It outshines all the pretty girls.

Neighbors whisper, 'What's that thing?'
A clasp of joy that makes hearts sing.
It jiggles on a coat so bright,
And brings a grin, a merry sight.

With every step, a jingle plays,
It leads the way through sunny days.
A curious charm, we all can see,
Who knew a pin could bring such glee?

Fragments of Hope

On a chilly day, a glimmer found,
A shiny gem that spins around.
With every stride, it catches light,
A quirky charm, what a delight!

At the café, it steals the show,
It shines so bright, it steals the glow.
Spilled coffee, laughter fills the air,
That radiant piece without a care.

A flutter here, a jiggle there,
Each movement grants a silly flair.
It beeps and honks like a car's alarm,
This chatty piece is full of charm.

Amidst the crowd, there's laughter loud,
That sparkling jewel, it feels so proud.
With every glance, our spirits rise,
Who knew hope wore such funny ties?

Brilliance Unfurled

A pin of color on a gray day,
It whispers secrets in a sassy way.
With winks and nods, it leads the fun,
A sparkle turning frowns to sun.

At every party, it steals the scene,
Wobbling 'round like a party machine.
Lighthearted glints from each tiny bead,
It trips on joy with every bead.

When everyone's down and feeling blue,
It shows up late, saying, 'Here's some view!'
A quirky dance, it steals a glance,
And leads us all in a silly dance.

So raise your glass to that shiny flair,
The glowing prize that lingers there.
With laughter bright, we lift our cheer,
This jewel of joy brings us near.

Dazzling Memories

In the attic lies a shining gem,
A relic wrapped, oh where's the hem?
With stories clinging like soft silk thread,
It holds our laughs, the tales unsaid.

Once at prom, it took the stage,
Under the lights, it danced with rage.
A twirl, a flip, it flew so high,
A boisterous star in a shy guy's eye.

Grown-up now, we take a look,
At shiny trinkets in every nook.
With every sparkle, a laugh doth blend,
What glows together, stays as friends.

So here's to gems that make us smile,
Reminding us to cherish the while.
With humor wrapped around each light,
Memories sparkle, forever bright.

The Dance of Light

Where sparkles twirl in outfits bright,
A cha-cha jig, a funky flight.
The sunbeam trips on prancing toes,
While disco balls steal all the shows.

With glimmers bouncing off the floor,
We giggle 'til our bellies sore.
In this cheerful, wobbly throng,
We laugh and dance the whole night long.

Illuminated Memories

Grandma's pearls, a sparkly tale,
She wore them while she'd giggle and wail.
Each shimmer holds a tale to tell,
Of silly moments, all is well.

We wore them once to chase a cat,
She hid behind the fancy mat.
Of all the glints and gleamy hues,
Our laughter sparkled like morning dew.

Threads of Luminescence

A tapestry of glittered strands,
Woven by mischievous hands.
We tried to make a cloak of cheer,
But turned it into a disco gear.

Those threads danced wildly, full of glee,
As we twirled 'round the old oak tree.
With every spin, a chuckle rang,
The clothes we donned, a funny clang.

The Brilliance in Shadows

Under the moon, shadows prance,
They sway and twist in a shadow dance.
The glow bugs giggle as they light,
Creating a ruckus in the night.

Their radiant gleam gives us a spree,
As we stumble trying to flee.
In gloom, our silliness shines bright,
Who knew we'd play, till morning light?

The Brightness in Between

In the middle of the day, a sparkle.
A cat runs by, chasing its tail.
I trip on my laces, it's a debacle,
But I laugh so hard, I can't fail.

Mismatched socks dance in pure glee,
Twinkling lights strung on a tree.
I throw confetti to the breeze,
And who knew that joy comes with a sneeze?

A sunbeam plays tag with my hat,
The neighbors stare; it's all in good fun.
I trip again, but how about that?
Even shadows want to run.

In this light-filled realm, I'm the queen,
Grinning wide from ear to ear.
Between the giggles, there's a sheen,
Life's a joke — and oh, so dear!

Kisses of Light upon the Soul

A wink from the sun, what a tease,
It laughs as the clouds cover my plans.
I dance like a fool, swaying with ease,
In the kitchen with spatula in hands.

Butterflies wearing polka-dot hats,
Fly upside down, it's a riotous sight.
They giggle like kids — where are the chats?
While I'm trying to catch them in flight.

Light tickles my cheeks, oh so bright,
I jump on a scale, what a shock!
Floating in joy, I take flight,
In a world where even rocks talk.

With every giggle, I feel it unfold,
A subtle nudge from the sun above.
Life's little quirks never grow old,
Shimmering laughter — oh, how I love!

Where Shadows Dance with Light

In a hallway where shadows prance,
They play peek-a-boo like silly elves.
The lamp flickers, and I take a chance,
To join in the game — forget myself.

With all the dance moves I can muster,
A cha-cha here, a slide over there.
I stumble on feet, oh, what a buster,
But the shadows just laugh, they don't care.

They twirl and swipe, a funny routine,
As I mimic every silly twist.
Caught in a gleam, I feel like a queen,
Yet find myself tangled in a mist.

Together we play, no need for grace,
In this theater of joy, all is bright.
Shadows and I, we've found our place,
Where laughter and light take fight!

Echoes of a Luminous Past

I found a vintage lightbulb today,
Wrapped in cobwebs, it giggled at me.
I plugged it in, it jumped in a sway,
Sending shadows into wild jubilee.

With a flashback to parties of yore,
Dancing socks on the ceiling with flair.
Balloons drift by, wanting more,
I'm stuck in this timewarp, I swear.

It weaves tales of glow sticks and fun,
Of crazy outfits and music so loud.
Beneath the flicker, a new day begun,
As I find my groove in this mad crowd.

And while the echoes of laughter stay,
I tip my hat to those times, so bright.
For the moments of joy chase gray away,
In this glorious rumble of light!

Beneath the Glare of Destiny

In a drawer where lost things hide,
Lies a pin that once had pride.
It sparkled bright, oh what a show,
Now it's just a rusted bow.

Once adorned by a lady fair,
Now it plays with dust and air.
'Twas a warrior, brave sort of plight,
Now it makes an excellent kite.

A conversation piece, it claims,
But all it does is play old games.
Telling tales of yesteryear,
As I'm pretending to appear.

So I wear it on a whim,
And watch my friends laugh on a whim.
With every glance, they ask for clues,
But all I've got are dusty shoes.

Glistening in Shadows

In shadows deep, a shimmer plays,
It winks and twirls in silly ways.
Is it a jewel or just a joke?
A sparkly thing on a rabbit's cloak.

I found it once in Grandma's room,
Among the dust and old perfume.
She said, 'That's magic, mind the leaks,'
But honestly, it just squeaks.

On coat lapels and tattered hats,
It dazzles like a bunch of gnats.
Everyone asks about its flair,
But really, who knows what's under there?

Decorated by tales so grand,
Of tangoing mice and a weird band.
But in reality, it's just delight,
A silly gem that sparkles bright.

The Radiance of Forgotten Tales

In an attic, stories sleep,
Shiny dreams that do not creep.
A formless glow of ancient glee,
Whispers secrets, wants to flee.

Remembered days in silver spun,
Of kittens playing, oh what fun!
Each glimmer hints at laughter past,
Yet present sparkles fade so fast.

They say it once was worn in style,
But now it sits, collecting guile.
A laughable relic of brighter times,
Where silliness laughs and simply chimes.

So don it proudly, embrace the jest,
For in the light, we are all blessed.
It tells a tale of gentle cheer,
And brings a smile to all who're near.

Secrets Woven in Silver

A glinting knot in fabric tight,
Whispers giggles in warm sunlight.
It once was bold, now found in grime,
Living for stories, carefree rhyme.

Each twist and turn held a delight,
Of pranks and jokes that took to flight.
Yet now it lies, a treasure mute,
A comic sight, like a lion's suit.

In gatherings, it starts a show,
With stories made from highs and lows.
Is it a charm or just a dare?
With every glance, we stop and stare.

So in this jumble, wear it proud,
Let laughter rise, shout it loud!
For in the silver, joy is spun,
And life's a joke, let's have some fun!

Flickers of Euphoria

A spark from the pocket, oh what a delight,
It dances and wiggles, quite a funny sight.
I swear it's alive, a mischievous grin,
It tickles the air, where does it begin?

With a jingle and jangle, it steals the show,
My friends just laugh, they can't help but glow.
In the game of the night, it's the wild card,
With giggles and smiles, we lower our guard.

It flickers and flutters, unpredictable spree,
A little bit of chaos, just you and me.
We'll chase down the giggles, hunt down the gleam,
With pockets of whimsy, we're lost in a dream.

So join in the fun, let the giggles ignite,
A spark of delight, we'll dance through the night.
For in every flicker, a story is spun,
In the laughter we share, we're always the one.

A Lighthouse of Hope

There's a beacon that shines, like a clown on parade,
Wobbling and bobbing, what mischief it made.
With a flicker of charm, it shouts from the shore,
"Here's hope and laughter, come get some more!"

In storms of confusion, it's never afraid,
With a giggle of twilight, the darkness will fade.
It winks at the ships, saying, "Come take a ride!"
With humor as compass, we'll sail side by side.

Oh yes, it's a lighthouse, but not just a guide,
A jester in glow, with joy as its pride.
When the waves come a-laughing, and the skies roll with glee,
We'll dance on the deck, just you wait and see.

So hoist up the flags, let the laughter ensue,
With a lighthouse of humor, we'll shine bright and true.
In the night's gentle hush, may our spirits arise,
With beams of pure joy, let's color the skies!

Luminescent Bonds

A glow in the crowd, oh how it amuses,
We're tangled in laughter, caught up in the fuses.
With winks and a nudge, we spark up the night,
Our friendship's a lantern, burning so bright.

Like lightning bugs buzzing, we flit to and fro,
Creating a dance that puts on quite a show.
In silly old stories, we find our delight,
Each giggle a thread that just feels so right.

Through tickles and jests, our bonds only grow,
A tapestry woven with warmth in the flow.
With every shared joke, we break down the walls,
In this luminescent dance, our laughter calls.

So grab on to joy, let it light up the way,
For with each little chuckle, we brighten the day.
Together we shine, in the fun and the cheer,
In these luminescent bonds, we never know fear.

Chiaroscuro Whispers

In shadows that flicker, whispers weave tales,
Of pranks and of jokes like wind in the sails.
With light and with laughter, we dance through the gloom,
A sketch of joy drawn, in a silly costume.

The jesters are laughing, oh what fun they'll bring,
With shadows in tow, they twirl and they sing.
"Let's light up the room, make the giggles collide!"
In the chiaroscuro, let our secrets slide.

Each flicker a story, when shadows take flight,
Laughter the canvas, our hearts burning bright.
With whispers of humor, we'll color the night,
In this playful ballet, all wrongs turn to right.

So hush now, dear friends, let the laughter bloom,
In the chiaroscuro, we conquer the gloom.
For in every chuckle, and every surprise,
We find our own magic, in whimsical skies.

Horizons of Glow

The sun peeks out, a cheeky sprite,
Chasing shadows, igniting delight.
With giggles and rays, it starts to play,
Painting the world in a bright ballet.

Clouds wear smiles in fluffy attire,
As the sky's palette bursts with fire.
Each blade of grass does a little jig,
While the breeze sings sweet like a playful gig.

Birds chirp jokes in the morning hue,
A feathered stand-up, just for you.
They swoop and swirl, with such a flair,
Filling the air with laughter to share.

So let your heart dance, don't hold it tight,
In life's vibrant canvas, find your light.
With every chuckle, let worries drift,
As the day unveils its joyful gift.

A Charm of Daybreak

Waking up with the sun's warm grin,
A dance of light, let the fun begin!
Coffee brews like a bubbling potion,
Fueling smiles and joyful motion.

The rooster crows with a jaunty sound,
As laughter echoes all around.
With pancakes flipping and syrup flowing,
Start the day with giggles glowing!

The flowers nod, dressed in their finest,
While bees buzz jokes with a cheeky kindness.
In this garden of morning bliss,
A sprinkle of humor, nothing amiss!

So gather your mates, it's a bright parade,
In shades of joy, let worries fade.
Every moment's a chance for glee,
As we embrace this day, wild and free.

Radiance in Stillness

In the hush of dusk, a soft glow gleams,
Whispers of light through the quiet dreams.
Even shadows wear a silly hat,
As the moon chuckles, 'Look where I'm at!'

Stars twinkle like they're playing cards,
Making wishes with their glistening shards.
The crickets share their nighttime tunes,
Quietly cracking up beneath the moon.

With fireflies joining the evening dance,
Each flicker a wink, a playful chance.
Nature's comedy plays in the night,
As darkness giggles and leans into light.

So find a spot and soak it in,
Let the hilarity of calm begin.
For in the stillness, joy's quite a sight,
A laugh in the shadows, oh what a delight!

The Luminary's Caress

A cheeky glow spills over the hill,
As the sun whispers, 'I'm here, what a thrill!'
With rays that tickle and warm your skin,
Daylight's laughter, let the fun begin!

Trees sway gently, with leaves all a-shimmer,
As squirrels pull pranks, that's their real winner.
They chatter jokes from limb to limb,
Each acorn a punchline on a whim!

The sun dips low with a glowing sigh,
Painting the sky in hues that fly.
In the twilight's chuckle, we find our peace,
A moment of mirth, as worries cease.

So bask in the glow, don't rush away,
In life's funny scenes, choose to play.
For every shimmer is a reason to cheer,
Embracing the joy that shines ever near.

A Veil of Illumination

In a land where the blinkers do glow,
A critter named Larry stole the show,
He wore a fine pin, or so he claimed,
But it twinkled too bright, and his friends were inflamed.

With glimmers and sparkles, it danced all around,
The squirrels were dazzled, and cats lost their ground,
But poor little Larry, he tripped on a vine,
And his precious shininess fell like confetti divine.

A dog spotted shimmer and ran with delight,
Chasing the glitter that sparkled at night,
Larry chased after, slipping and sliding,
His shine was a beacon, his laughter was blinding.

In antics and laughter, he gathered his crew,
Wearing a crown made of nothing but goo,
They danced under stars, each twinkling apart,
For in moments of folly, they all found the art!

A Starlit Message

In the night sky, stars start to twinkle,
A cosmic dance, with a wink and a sprinkle.
Aliens giggle from their craft with delight,
Sending clumsy signals, oh what a sight!

A comet sneezes, spreading starlight dust,
While astronauts chuckle, they're filled with such trust.
Messages float from Venus to Mars,
"Send more tacos, we're short on snacks, guys!"

Each twinkle broadcasts a secret or two,
"Hey Charlie! Bring pizza, we're starving, it's true!"
The Milky Way's laughter echoes so bright,
In a universe full of pure cosmic light!

So next time you gaze at the night sky's glow,
Remember the chuckles you cannot quite know.
For stars are more than just sparkles and glow,
They're mischief-makers with laughter in tow!

Reflections of the Heart

Mirrors are laughing with each little glance,
Showing our style in a wobbly dance.
Lipstick catastrophe, and hair gone awry,
'Is that really me?' we all wonder why!

Each heartbeat echoes a tune so absurd,
"Did I just trip over that stray little bird?"
Love's a funny thing, a playful charade,
Like pie in the face that we all hope won't fade.

Glances exchanged, with a wink and a grin,
Two hearts on this ride, let the laughter begin!
With each silly moment, we cherish the most,
It's the joy of the heart that we love to toast.

So let's raise a glass to our ups and our downs,
To the giggles and grins and the wobbly crowns.
For in this grand journey of hilarity's art,
We find all the beauty in reflections of heart!

Glorious Radiance

In a world full of bling, one gem stands apart,
Sparkling so brightly, it wins every heart.
Worn by the squirrel in a dashing parade,
With laughter and joy, it's brightly displayed!

Frogs try to steal it with their slippery charm,
While butterflies giggle, they mean no real harm.
Each sparkle that glimmers brings chuckles galore,
As it rolls down the hill, what a bumbling chore!

"Fetch that jewel!" yells a raccoon in the night,
But it's just rolling away in pure delight.
With each little bounce, it sings songs of cheer,
A hilarious chase, oh dear, oh dear!

So if you find jewels, let laughter be free,
And wear your own sparkle, let's dance by the tree.
For in every shimmer and radiant show,
The funniest moments are what we bestow!

The Glimmering Dream

In dreams, there's much sparkle, a fanciful flight,
Where penguins wear tuxedos and dance through the night.
Rainbows spill jellybeans across the sky,
And giraffes tell jokes that make everyone cry!

A unicorn giggles, "Hey, check out my mane!"
While mermaids are singing a tune in the rain.
With each twinkling vision that dances around,
The laughter we share is hilariously sound!

Monkeys with glasses are solving great truths,
While elephants skate with the slickest of moves.
The silliness swirls like a relentless stream,
In this wacky, whimsical, glimmering dream!

So hold onto your pillows, let laughter take flight,
For these comical visions bring joy to the night.
In slumbers where giggles and sparkles align,
We find silly wonder in realms full of shine!

Celestial Adornments

Stars wore hats to dance at night,
A comet's tail took flight!
The moon giggled, round and bright,
While planets played a game of fright.

Saturn's rings spun like a hula,
While Neptune played the ukulele,
Mars wore lipstick, quite a stunner,
And Venus cooked up cosmic fun, oh what a hummer!

A meteor crashed with a splash,
It slipped on stardust, oh what a clash!
Galaxies laughed at this show,
Who knew space could steal the glow?

In a nebula, they held a feast,
With glowing soup, the brightest, least!
They toasted with sparkling Milky Way,
Yelling, "Here's to another flashy day!"

Luminary Legacy

A bright light took a stroll one night,
It tripped over a satellite,
Bouncing back, it giggled with glee,
"Is this how stars all find their spree?"

The sun wore shades, looking so cool,
While meteors raced, "We rule this school!"
A solar wind brushed past so bold,
Telling secrets the stars once told.

"Did you hear about that bright new star?"
It called to the others, "Oh my, what a bazaar!"
They chuckled and twinkled in the dark,
Wishing their comets would make a spark.

Memory of stardust slipped through space,
Leaving behind a giggling trace,
In this legacy of light and fun,
Every glow was just so begun!

Twinkle in the Shadows

In the corners where shadows play,
A wink from a star would light the way,
"Hey there!" it called with a twinkling grin,
"Catch me if you can, let the games begin!"

Planets peeked round a cosmic bend,
Hiding secrets they meant to send,
A black hole chuckled, "Not today, my friend,
I'll swallow your light till the very end!"

Stars played hide and seek with the comets,
While asteroids tossed around like lil' rockets,
The moon rolled over, laughing so wide,
Saying, "Writing my name in the night sky is my pride!"

Elves of light came out to cheer,
Their laughter echoed for all to hear,
In this space of playful delight,
Even the shadows sparkled bright!

Illuminated Dreams

A starry sleeper took a nap,
Dreamed of jazz with a twinkling clap,
Dancing brought galaxies to play,
As they sang until the break of day.

In dreams, the sun wore a party hat,
While starlight kittens purred, "Imagine that!"
They brewed some comet stew for their snack,
Cosmic doughnuts on a celestial rack.

Twinkling wishes floated like feathers,
Sprinkling laughter like party sweaters,
"Time for fun," whispered the night,
Turning dreams into pure delight.

A moonlit dance was all the rage,
Every star turned a brand new page,
In this nighttime circus of beams,
The universe laughed in illuminated dreams!

Reflections of a Shimmering Soul

In a world so bright and merry,
The gems all danced, oh so contrary.
One said, "I shine like no other!"
The next replied, "Well, let's not smother!"

With sparkles flying here and there,
They laughed and twinkled without a care.
A diamond claimed to be the best,
But a joke was all he could ingest!

They spun around in a dazzling race,
But tripped on glitter—oh, what a face!
With every tumble, they would gleam,
As giggles burst apart the dream!

In playful jests, they found their cheer,
A shimmering crew without any fear.
In laughter's light, they formed their goal,
To brighten hearts and lift the soul!

Threads of Luminescence

Tangled threads of light and hue,
Weaving tales, both old and new.
A slip of silk, a colorful thread,
Made every story dance and spread!

"Do you see my shine?" one thread would boast,
While others laughed, now that's a roast!
With twirls and knots, they showed their flair,
In stitches of humor beyond compare.

One thread tripped on its own fine lace,
Falling in style, a comical grace!
The others giggled, "What a fine show!"
"To be that bright, you've got to get low!"

Together they sparkled, a quilt of glee,
Crafting laughter by the yard, you see?
In every twist, a joke to unfurl,
Threads of sunbeams in a joyful whirl!

Chronicles of Dazzling Light

Once upon a time in a beam,
A story spun like a whimsical dream.
The stars all gathered for a fun chat,
"Who's the shiniest?" said one little brat.

One said, "My twinkle will make you squint!"
Another replied, "I'll give you a hint!"
With giggles bright, they played all night,
Creating tales of pure delight.

A comet zoomed with a gleeful cheer,
"I'm a speedster, I've got no fear!"
But a meteor, clumsy and spry,
Fell flat on the sun—oh my, oh my!

Through bursts of laughter in the sky,
They filled the cosmos, oh what a high!
In every spark, a chuckle flowed,
Chronicles of light, where joy bestowed!

The Luster Beneath the Surface

Beneath the sheen and glowing face,
Lurked a tale of giggles in space.
"One day," said a gem, "I lost my shine,
And ended up in a bowl of brine!"

"Oh dear!" cried another, "What a plight!
But you still sparkle in the moonlight!"
They rolled with laughter, a merry crew,
Finding humor in what they'd been through.

A pearl chimed in with a wink,
"Being dull at times makes you think!
Without the depth, what fun would life be?
Let's all glow, just silly and free!"

Together they shimmered, reflecting cheer,
Dancing in shadows, no hint of fear.
In every wink and giggle they'd find,
The luster of laughter intertwined!

Spark of Belief

In the pocket where dreams can hide,
A shiny thing, it sits with pride.
With a wink and a jolly grin,
It's said to make you dance and spin.

A sprinkle of hope, it claims to bring,
Transforming mundane into a swing.
But when I put it to the test,
I tripped and stumbled; what a jest!

It glints and glimmers, so they say,
Yet sent my cat scurrying away.
With every sparkle, laughter flows,
Reflecting joy—who really knows?

So keep your treasures, hidden tight,
For magic lives in the silly light.
In laughter shared, we might just see,
The shine that sets our spirits free.

Enigma of Light

There's a thing that shines, a cryptic clue,
That tickles thoughts of me and you.
With every flash, a riddle forms,
And laughter spills like summer storms.

A twinkle here, a shimmer there,
It plays a game—do we dare share?
I tried to grasp its fleeting glow,
But lost my balance, much to my woe!

It holds the secrets of delight,
Yet left me wrapped in giggles tight.
A joke concealed in the glimmering,
What folly comes from this funny bling?

With whispers soft and cheeky tease,
This puzzling charm brings me to my knees.
In every chuckle, we align,
As shadows dance in silly design.

Enshrouded Brilliance

In a closet dark, a secret gleams,
Draped in fabric, tangled dreams.
When pulled out, it winks with glee,
A caper wrapped in mystery.

They say it's magic, a radiant gift,
But my hopes collided with a misfit.
It sparkled bright, like a neon sign,
Then led me straight into the brine!

With every flicker, a giggle breaks,
As I slip and slide on all the flakes.
A target for glances, a jest in flight,
Chasing shadows till the morning light.

So congregate, all friends so dear,
For brilliance sings when we all cheer.
In tangled tales and a playful spree,
We bask in the glow of our revelry.

Glistening Reverie

A twinkling gem, it calls my name,
With playful thoughts, it's never lame.
In whimsical dreams where sparkles flare,
I wear my joy, with style and flair.

Though friends may tease, I hold it high,
Dancing in circles, as time flies by.
With every shine, a story told,
Of silly antics and laughter bold.

It jests about fortune, a comic fit,
With a wink and a nudge, it's quite a hit!
In the glow of laughter, mishaps come,
As we stumble 'round, oh what fun!

So let us toast to glimmers bright,
In friendship shared, we'll take flight.
For in this reverie of gleeful bliss,
We find ourselves in the sparkle's kiss.

Fragments of a Prismed Dream

In a world of sparkles, we trip and slide,
Chasing rainbows on a merry ride.
With our mismatched socks and wild hair,
We laugh at shadows that wait somewhere.

A cat in a cape, a dog with a hat,
Dancing in circles, imagine that!
Underneath the disco ball's glow,
Finding joy in each silly show.

Puddles reflect our squeaky shoes,
Jumping and splashing, we can't lose!
Our whispers echo, secrets shared,
In the prismed dream, we all dared.

With every giggle, colors combine,
Creating a laughter no one can confine.
So let's spin in circles, let joy ignite,
In this fractal fun, we'll shine so bright.

Glows of Remembrance Cascading

From granny's closet, a treasure I find,
A necklace of mismatched stones, so unrefined.
With jangly laughter and silly grins,
We wear our past like brightly spun sins.

Oh, Uncle Joe with his wild old tales,
Tells of mermaids with glittery scales.
We giggle and shrug, he's a legend, you see,
In our memory, he's as grand as can be!

As we cascade down mind's slippery lane,
Caught in the glow of nostalgic rain.
Each droplet a sparkle, each laugh a delight,
An illumination of wrong and of right.

So toast to the moments that make us whole,
With clinks of our glasses, we capture the soul.
For in every gleam, a story cascades,
In the glows of remembrance, joy never fades.

A Tapestry of Starry Glimmers

In the night sky, the stars start to play,
Knitting up dreams that twinkle away.
A cosmic quilt with threads of delight,
As we dance through the darkness, chasing the light.

Captured in stardust, we fall and we rise,
Whispers of laughter, surprises in guise.
Every twinkle a secret, no need for a chart,
Just follow the giggles, that's where we start.

Mom says we're silly, we just can't agree,
With tinfoil hats, we plot our decree.
We'll weave in some laughter, throw sparkles around,
As we conquer the cosmos from this very ground.

So bring out the crayons, let's color the void,
With strokes of our humor, we'll never be bored.
In this tapestry woven with starry glimmers,
Who knew the night's laughter could make our hearts shimmer?

The Light that Adorns the Void

In an empty room, we discovered the fun,
With shadows and giggles, our adventure begun.
Each flicker of light casts goofy grins,
Creating a landscape where mischief begins.

We chase after beams like they're ice cream cones,
Sliding on laughter, no need for cell phones.
Dancing with shadows that stretch and yawn,
Until we collapse at the break of dawn.

Oh, the void's just a canvas for our playful art,
With doodles of joy drawn straight from the heart.
So let's brighten the corners with zany delight,
For in every giggle, we conquer the night.

With pinwheels and wishes, let's spin 'til we drop,
In this game in the dark, we'll never stop.
For the light that we share is a joke yet untold,
In the void, we've found treasures more precious than gold.

A Light's Journey

A spark on a quest, oh what a sight,
Chasing shadows, bidding them goodnight.
Through kitchens and gardens, it twirls with glee,
Tickling the noses of folks like me.

It bounced on the walls, made friends with the cat,
Danced on the fridge, left a note on the mat.
'Where's my next gig?' it beams with delight,
A party for socks, oh, what a fine night!

Its journey continues, around every bend,
Shining in corners where dust bunnies blend.
A flash in the hallway, a wink in the dark,
Lampshades all giggle as they join in the spark.

Oh light, you're a fool, but we love your plight,
Chasing our hearts like it's one fun-filled flight.
With quirky adventures, where chaos is rife,
You shine like a champ, and you're loving this life!

An Ode to Radiance

Oh luminary spark, with a wink and a grin,
You flicker and flutter, spreading cheer within.
You play peekaboo with a mop in the hall,
While the dog barks at shadows that leap off the wall.

You glimmer on spoons at breakfast's grand feast,
And light up the puddles, calling friends to the east.
The toaster, it chuckles, as you shine all around,
Inviting the crumbs to a waltz on the ground.

You're the star of the jokes, a radiance prank,
Turning lampshades to hats, oh how the light sank!
You tickle the curtains while they flutter and sway,
Creating a party in the mid-afternoon play.

So here's to your glow, that brightens our day,
The laughter you bring in each quirky display.
You shine with such charm, bringing smiles to all,
Our whimsical beacon, forever enthralled!

Prismatic Journeys

In prisms of laughter, we travel afar,
With hues so vibrant, they twinkle like stars.
A blue one named Buster loves to tell jokes,
While red, the wise elder, just giggles and pokes.

They bounce on the walls, in a playful parade,
Tickling silence with colors, not afraid.
Through kitchens and lounges, the hues dance about,
Turning the mundane into a rave, there's no doubt!

A swirl of bright giggles, a flash of good cheer,
Our gang of bright colors is always near.
They steal the stage lights, making shadows collide,
While painting the world with their radiant pride.

So let's raise a toast to this colorful spree,
With laughter and joy, they set our hearts free.
For on this bold journey, with hues side by side,
Life sparkles in laughter, a luminous ride!

Hues of Illumination

In shades of bright hues, the fun never stops,
A rainbow of chuckles in giggly drops.
A green light named Clover swings wide on the beam,
While purple named Berry plays tag with a dream.

They waltz through the kitchen, then zip down the hall,
Painting each corner with laughter for all.
The ceilings are laughing as colors do leap,
Awakening joy from a wonderful sleep.

A twinkle, a shimmer, they sparkle and dash,
Over lamps, 'round the chairs, in one glorious flash.
With a wink and a grin, they cheerfully call,
'Join in the fun—come and dance, one and all!'

So here's to the hues that brighten our fate,
With a humor so light, it never feels late.
In the world of illumination, we surely concur,
That laughter and color are life's sweetest blur!

Glimmering Pathways of Destiny

In a garden where twinkling things play,
There's a cat wearing sparkles, bright as the day.
He prances with style, a crown on his head,
Chasing fireflies round where no one else tread.

A squirrel in shades, looking quite debonair,
Dances on branches, without a single care.
He nabs all the acorns, keeps them in line,
While humming a tune with a slight silly twine.

The moon tips its hat to a waltzing bee,
Buzzing along with a dance so carefree.
He twirls 'neath the stars, feeling light as a feather,
As the witty raccoons cheer him on, together.

Through laughter and giggles, they all take the lead,
In a whimsical world where no one pays heed.
Paths glitter with joy, as they stumble and roll,
In the glimmering madness, they find heart and soul.

The Glow of Hearts Entwined

Two hearts in a tangle, like yarn gone astray,
Trying to knit a warm blanket of play.
They trip over laughter, they giggle and fall,
Knitting together the silliest wall.

A dog in a bonnet, prancing with pride,
Stealing the sneakers from those who abide.
He wags his tail fiercely, a quirky delight,
As the shoes chase their owner through laughter's bright night.

A bird in a tutu, with feathers all bright,
Ballets in circles, a whimsical sight.
With a wink and a smile, he twirls to the ground,
As the crowd of his friends emits cheers all around.

Together they shine, like stars in the sky,
In a merry fandango where whimsies fly high.
Hearts glowing with humor, their spirits aligned,
Finding joy in their chaos, beautifully combined.

Glimmers of Radiance

A frog in a jacket, so dapper and green,
Hops from a lily, the quirkiest scene.
With a wink and a splash, he declares, "Take a leap!"
Springing through marshes where giggles run deep.

A turtle on skates zooms by in a whirl,
Shouting, "Catch me if you can, give it a twirl!"
He zips past the flowers, they laugh at his pace,
While butterflies join in this raucous race.

The sun wears a top hat, shining so bright,
Giving hugs to the daisies, bathing in light.
With each silly bow, all the blooms start to sway,
In a rhythm of joy, they dance through the day.

And when evening approaches, the stars start to play,
With wishes of goofballs in foolish ballet.
In the glimmers of laughter, they dance through the night,

Creating a canvas of pure, silly light.

Shimmering Secrets

In a glade where the giggles are ever so loud,
A hedgehog with sparkles stands out from the crowd.
He whispers sweet secrets to those passing by,
Wearing sneakers and shades, oh my, oh my!

A rabbit in bow ties, flicks his long floppy ear,
Says, "Join my tea party! There's cake and good cheer!"
With teacups of laughter and pie made of dreams,
In a world of delight, or so so it seems.

Butterflies gossip, paint stories on air,
Their fluttering tales twirling in light, so rare.
They swoop like acrobats through glitter-filled skies,
Mischief and charm dance in each one's eyes.

The night wraps around them like snug little blankets,
With wishes in whispers tucked under the trinkets.
All secrets of joy are shared with a kiss,
In shimmering moments, they find perfect bliss.

Shimmering Threads of Dawn

In the morning's playful cheer,
A ribbon twirls, oh what a steer!
Dancing shadows, laughter spry,
As sunlight flirts from way up high.

With sparkles bouncing off the wall,
It tickles, makes the curtains fall.
The cat, it pounces, what a sight,
Chasing beams of golden light.

As tea brews up with fragrant steam,
I catch a glimpse, or is it a dream?
That little shimmer on the floor,
Whispers secrets, begs for more.

We glide and slip, we laugh and spin,
In this morning's joyful din.
What treasures hide in every ray,
A dance of shadows here to stay.

Luminescent Whispers of Hope

Underneath the kitchen sink,
A speck of light begins to blink.
Is it a bug? A gleaming flea?
Nah, just my missing cup of tea!

With frothy laughter, we decree,
That glimmer gives us all a spree.
Wobbling mugs, a toast in jest,
To twinkling hopes, we are so blessed!

In the garden, the gnomes have fun,
They think that they can outshine the sun.
With cheeks so round, and hats so tall,
They giggle, waiting for a fall.

A wink, a nudge, the flowers bloom,
Each petal holds a tale of gloom.
Yet in this laughter, fears take flight,
As whispers turn to vivid light.

The Gemstone's Secret Glow

In a drawer, where socks collide,
A little gem begins to hide.
It giggles soft, its shine discreet,
Among the cotton, oh what a feat!

It winks at me as I dig deep,
For mismatched socks I cannot keep.
Is it a treasure, or just a joke?
It twirls around like some wild smoke.

A sparkle here, a glimmer there,
The mystery of their playful flair.
Do they conspire, or mock my plight?
In laughter's hue, they feel so right!

With every chuckle from my chest,
I grasp the gem, oh what a jest!
It spins, it twirls, it beams so bright,
My little secret in the night.

Radiant Echoes of Yesterday

In the attic where old hats lay,
A twinkling past begins to play.
With dusty hats and shoes unpaired,
Oh, what adventures had they dared!

The echo of a jester's cheer,
A memory draws us, brings us near.
Laughter trapped in wooden beams,
Reveals itself through playful dreams.

As sunlight floods this timeless space,
The whispers dance, the giggles race.
Holding hands, we spin and sway,
In radiant echoes, we play all day!

"Is that a ghost?" I whisper light,
"No, just the past in sheer delight!"
Together we make shadows cast,
In laughter's warmth, we're free at last.

Reflections of Brilliance

In a world of shiny things,
I wore a gem that laughs and sings.
It twinkled bright, a cheeky glare,
And made the sun feel quite the glare.

My friends all stared, their jaws agape,
As I paraded like a grape.
They said, 'What's that? A star gone wrong?'
I winked and danced, just sang my song.

But in the night, it shone much clearer,
The moonlight made my look much dearer.
A disco ball upon my chest,
With every move, I felt the best!

So here's to jewels that bring us cheer,
To funny moments we hold dear.
In laughter's light, we boldly flaunt,
Our sparkles grand, with cheeky taunt.

Aeon of Light

Once I found a shiny piece,
It claimed to bring eternal peace.
I wore it once, it slipped and fell,
Now it's wedged beneath the shell.

A glowing grin upon my face,
As I tripped and found a silly place.
The lights around began to pop,
They giggled loud; I couldn't stop.

Be careful where you let it roam,
It draws attention like a gnome.
I'd laugh so hard, I nearly choked,
While in the dark, my friends just joked.

In every twist, a funny catch,
This luminous friend? A perfect match.
We've lit the nights with our delight,
An endless dance of laughter's light.

The Ethereal Emblem

In my pocket lies a charm,
That spins and twirls, it brings me harm.
I took it out to show a friend,
It ricocheted 'round the bend.

The laughter echoed through the space,
As I tried to keep a straight face.
It buzzed and zapped like bumblebees,
Performing tricks that brought us to knees.

A flash of color, quick as light,
It made the tallest friend take flight.
'Who needs a crown?' they all would shout,
'When you can wear a sparkly bout?'

So here we stand, in humor's glow,
Our dear emblem steals the show.
For in each laugh, a bit of glee,
That sparkles bright in you and me.

Twilight's Embrace

At dusk, I found a trinket light,
That glimmered softly, oh so bright.
I wore it proudly, a funny sight,
As shadows danced in gleeful flight.

But oh, the way it made me trip,
In twilight's hug, I could not grip.
My friends all laughed, their faces wide,
As I became a glowing guide.

Through every twist and silly turn,
The gem would glimmer, brightly burn.
Yet all the while, I'd laugh, not pout,
In this wild game, there's no doubt.

With every flash, a giggle flew,
In twilight's arms, we found our crew.
So let's embrace this gleeful phase,
And shine together through the haze.

www.ingramcontent.com/pod-product-compliance
Lightning Source LLC
Chambersburg PA
CBHW060122230426
43661CB00003B/289